MARQUETRY

*To everyone who has helped and inspired
my work in marquetry.*

MARQUETRY

HOW TO MAKE PICTURES
AND PATTERNS IN WOOD VENEERS

David Hume

SEARCH PRESS

First published in Great Britain 1994

Search Press Limited
Wellwood, North Farm Road,
Tunbridge Wells, Kent TN2 3DR

Reprinted 1997, 2001

ISBN 0 85532 763 4

If you have difficulty in obtaining any of the materials
or equipment mentioned in this book, please write for
further information to the publishers.
Search Press Limited, Wellwood, North Farm Road,
Tunbridge Wells, Kent TN2 3DR, England

Printed by Elkar, S. Coop. 48180 Loiu, Spain

Page 1
Elm Street, Norwich
Size: 150 x 100mm (6 x 4in)

Page 3
Chaffinch
Size: 175 x 125mm (7 x 5in)

Page 5
Stalactites and stalagmites
Size: 250 x 135mm (10 x 5$\frac{1}{4}$in)

Contents

Late – seventeenth-century Dutch marquetry circular wine cooler, finely inlaid with flowers and foliage in boxwood.

INTRODUCTION

Marquetry is the art of using the colour and grain of wood veneers to create a picture which is overlaid on to a solid background.

Although it has become very popular in recent times–the range of kits available proves this point–few people realise that the art of veneering goes back thousands of years. As far back as 3500BC Egyptians used inlaid wood to decorate a harp; while hieroglyphics found in the Valley of the Kings show Egyptian craftsmen cutting veneers from logs. They were able to cut their veneers to about 6mm ($1/4$in) in thickness and used hand-grinders made of stone to smooth the veneers. They were also the first to glue their veneers on to thin sheets of common wood.

The art of veneering was nearly lost during the Dark Ages, but was revived early in the fourteenth century when intarsia panels were made to decorate cathedrals in northern Italy. The panels were in the form of pictures made from veneers, and depicted biblical scenes, figures of saints, buildings and courtyards.

Veneers used in these panels were 3–4mm (about $1/8$in) thick–much thicker than the modern ones. They were cut using a shoulder knife; so called because the wooden handle, placed against the shoulder, acted as a fulcrum to enable the whole weight of the body to be applied to the knife blade and assist in the cutting operation.

By the late fourteenth century, motifs depicting a wide range of subjects, from landscapes to figures and inlaid banding, were to be seen on solid walnut furniture made in Urbino, Bologna, Verona and Naples. Geometric inlays were also used on Spanish furniture in the sixteenth century.

In 1562 the fretsaw was invented in Germany and this enabled two contrasting veneers to be cut at the same time. In Germany, ebony cabinets were decorated with arabesque marquetry, while in France André Charles Boulle used tortoise-shell and brass on his ebony cabinets.

Several styles of veneering arrived in England, brought to the country first from Italy and then, when Elizabeth I came to the throne, by Flemish craftsmen. They were subsequently followed by the French, in 1572, who produced furniture made from walnut and ebony decorated with marquetry. From 1660 floral marquetry was used extensively on panels; then oyster parquetry was introduced, and this was used in border surrounds.

The baroque style gave way to foliated acanthus marquetry, known as seaweed marquetry, which comprised scrolls of boxwood and holly inlaid into walnut in an arabesque style. The use of marquetry then declined until Robert Adams reintroduced it in the eighteenth century; he used sand shading for his semi-circular fans, shell inlays and other motifs on his furniture.

After 1818, when the first veneer slicer was invented by Henry Faveryear, logs could be cut to obtain the best 'figure' on the veneer with a lot less waste.

Small Dutch eighteenth-century bow-fronted corner cupboard, decorated with floral designs in tulipwood and kingwood.

In the 1830s a different technique, later to be known as 'Tunbridge ware', came into use. Craftsmen used thin matchstick-like pieces of wood, of various types and colours, which they glued together as a block, forming a picture across the end of the block. The block was then sliced to produce a number of identical images – butterflies, birds, flowers, castles, houses and street scenes. The slices were used to decorate jewellery boxes, snuff boxes and tea caddies.

Between 1920 and 1940 wall panels became popular in restaurants, offices, banks and shops. Railway carriages were also decorated with panels, as were the passenger ships *Queen Mary* and *Queen Elizabeth*. One panel on the *Queen Elizabeth*, the 'Canterbury Pilgrims', measured 7.5 x 6 metres (24 x 20 feet).

The method of creating pictures from wood veneers has changed little over the centuries, although the variety and availability of veneers have increased. Cutting techniques have also improved. The fretsaw has generally been replaced by the craft knife. However, fretsaws are still used for cutting a large number of identically shaped pieces (usually for commercial production of inlay motifs). They must also be used for cutting thick veneers when restoring furniture. The methods of cutting with a fretsaw are covered extensively in other publications.

There are different ways of building up a picture from wood veneers but I have found that the 'window' method of cutting gives very successful results. I describe the techniques of this method on pages 20 and 21, and I use them in my step-by-step instructions.

I hope to show you that a newcomer to this craft can create interesting and exciting designs of his or her own. The book will also be useful to those who are already familiar with marquetry, but who wish to progress beyond commercial kits.

Inspiration for a design can be taken from a variety of sources and you will derive hours of enjoyment and satisfaction from translating designs into finished pictures.

Right: Detail from a walnut cabinet inlaid with satinwood, circa 1820.

TOOLS AND MATERIALS

On the following pages you can see the tools and materials used in marquetry. They are all readily available from most art and craft shops. I have given details about choosing cutting blades and general information about other tools and materials.

Tools and materials

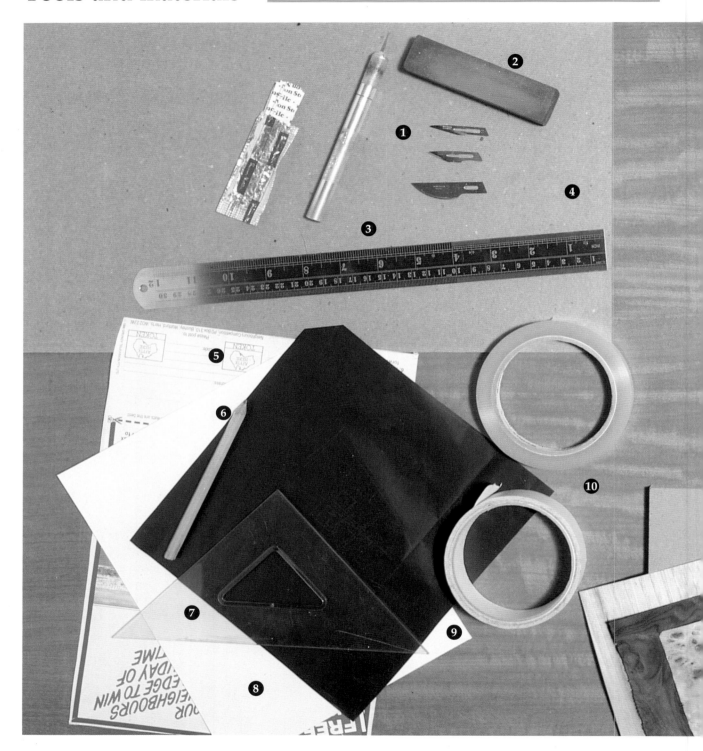

1. Knife handle with interchangeable blades.
2. Sharpening stone.
3. Steel ruler.
4. Cutting board.
5. Pieces of white card (wasters).
6. Pencil.
7. Set square.
8. Plain white paper.
9. Carbon paper.
10. Sticky tape.
11. PVA glue.
12. Contact adhesive.

13. Glue spreader.
14. Syringe.
15. Scraper.
16. Sanding papers and sanding block.

17. Sanding sealer.
18. Polish.
19. Mounting board.
20. Veneers.

21. Press (not illustrated).

Cutting tools

The most important item is the knife; there are a multitude of different types but the best ones for marquetry are those with interchangeable, very narrow blades that fit into a separate handle.

Knife handle: the type of handle is really down to personal choice. I prefer a round one which allows a certain amount of pressure without the sore finger I might get using a narrow handle.

Blades: narrow, sharp-pointed, straight scalpel blades are most suitable for cutting the individual pieces of the marquetry picture. A larger blade with a rounded edge is useful for cutting against a straight-edge when making borders, etc.

Sharpening stone

An oilstone is best, and you can buy them with a coarse grit on one side and a fine grit on the other.

It is very important to keep the knife blade sharp at all times. This will make the cutting process easier and will help avoid slips. Cutting veneers only dulls the tip of the blade and my method of keeping a sharp tip is to grind the back of the blade on an oil stone. Alternatively, you can use a sharpening stick made from a coarse abrasive paper glued to a piece of plywood or MDF (medium density fibreboard).

Keep the chamfered edge of the blade sharp by honing it with a fine grit paper.

Grind the back of the blade to keep it sharp.

Cutting board

Use a piece of firm but soft material, such as thick cardboard, lino, vinyl floor tiles or plywood. Alternatively you can buy a special self-healing cutting mat; these are relatively expensive but they will last for years if used correctly.

Ruler/straight-edge

You will need a ruler for sizing your picture and for measuring the borders, and a good straight-edge for cutting veneers. A steel ruler/straight-edge or a non-slip safety ruler are most suitable. Do not cut veneers against a plastic ruler.

Wasters

A waster is a piece of white card, slightly larger than the finished picture, used as a temporary background out of which the initial window shapes are cut. It needs to be roughly the same thickness as the veneers and I find that the sides of old cereal boxes are ideal.

Tracing equipment

You must trace the background details of your picture on to the waster and then progressively add more detail until the picture is complete. Carbon paper and a hard pencil give good sharp images; do not press too hard with the pencil, especially when tracing through on to veneers.

Adhesive tape

Use a low-tack type as a temporary measure to fix the veneers into the design. Hard, brittle veneers, which are likely to split when cutting, should also be taped along the edges to be cut. Masking tape can leave a residue of glue on the veneer, especially if left on for long periods.

Glues

PVA: this is the best glue for assembling and laying your picture. Although it is white in the liquid state it is transparent when dry and it is non-staining. Your finger is the best tool for applying glue when assembling the picture but you should use a spreader when laying down large areas of adhesive on to the backing board.

Use a spreader to lay large expanses of glue.

Impact- or contact-type adhesives: you will use these primarily for gluing edge veneers to the mounted picture. Do follow the manufacturer's instructions – you should apply a layer of adhesive to both the veneer and the baseboard, wait for the glue to dry and then stick the veneer in position.

Syringe

This is not an essential item but it is useful for inserting extra glue under any blisters in the finished picture (see page 22).

Finishing equipment

When you have completed the assembly of your picture and mounted it on a backing board, it must be 'finished' by flattening, sanding and polishing.

Scraper: this is a flat-bladed tool for reducing the thickness of some heavier veneers.

Sanding papers: you will need various grades of garnet or silicon carbide paper (180, 220, 280, and 320 grit sizes) together with a cork or wood sanding block.

Sanding sealer: apply a coat of cellulose or shellac sealer before you start the sanding operation and further coats during the finishing process.

Wax polish: finish the picture with one or two coats of a white siliconised furniture wax polish.

Baseboard

The best material for the baseboard is MDF (medium density fibreboard) which is very stable. If this is not available, a furniture-grade chipboard would be suitable. A piece 9mm ($^3/_8$in) thick is sufficient for all the pictures in this book. For larger pictures use either 12 or 18mm ($^1/_2$ or $^3/_4$in) thick boards.

Veneers

One particular tree can provide a variety of different types of veneer (see page 76). Many species of tree have the same common name but have completely different veneer characteristics.

I have illustrated and identified some of the veneers that I use regularly on pages 26 and 74.

Some of the highly figured veneers, especially butt and burr veneers, are available only in small sheet sizes and these can have small holes in them.

Stockists hold some veneers as consecutive sheets each of which have very similar grain patterns. Open these as you would pages of a book, and you get mirror images of grain to use in borders.

Part of a sheet of walnut butt veneer showing a small hole. This is a feature of butt and burr veneers that are cut from small and often knotty pieces of timber.

Making a simple press

If you use PVA for mounting your picture on to its backing board you will need some form of press. You could use a heavy weight, or a pile of books, but you can make a simple home-made press quite easily using the materials listed opposite.

Screw the bottom bearers to the bottom caul, equi-spaced down the long edge. The top bearers are shaped so that they taper from the centre to the outside and are secured to the frame with the bolts and wing nuts. The shape of the top bearers means that pressure is applied to the middle of the panel first, pushing any air and excess glue outwards to the edges of the picture.

To make the press you will need:
1. Two pieces of 18mm (³/₄in) thick blockboard or MDF, approximately 500 x 400mm (18 x 16in) in size, for the cauls (pressing boards).

2. Six or eight lengths of hardwood about 50 x 75 x 480mm (2 x 3 x 19in) for the bearers (clamps).

3. Six or eight 180mm (7in) long bolts together with wing nuts and washers.

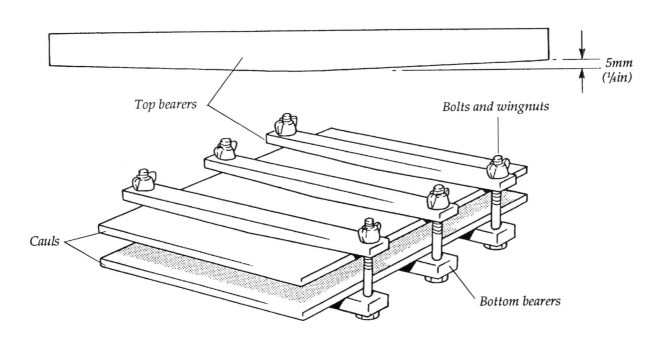

Top bearers

Bolts and wingnuts

5mm (¼in)

Cauls

Bottom bearers

BASIC SKILLS

Before getting down to making your first marquetry picture I suggest that you learn a few basic skills and techniques. You will need to know how to create a working design and to practise cutting techniques. I have also included details of how to remedy some of the common faults that can occur.

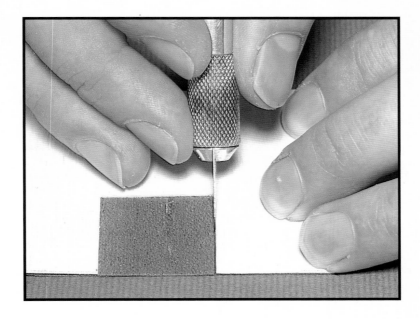

Designing a picture

There are many ways to obtain a design for a marquetry picture. Probably the first ones you use will be those supplied with the marquetry kits that are readily available from craft shops. However, there is nothing difficult about adapting any picture into a design for marquetry.

Look at pictures in books, magazines, calendars, postcards, etc., or even your own holiday snapshots. Of course, if you are artistically inclined, then the most obvious source is your own creativity.

Limitations on picture size

When you have chosen a particular picture to use you must then decide on the dimensions of the finished work.

This is an important consideration and you may be limited by the sheet size of a particular veneer. For example, the picture may have a large expanse of sky, water or background which, at the chosen size, will require a veneer larger than is available locally.

If you use PVA to glue your picture to the backing board you must also consider the size of press available to you.

Working design

When you have chosen your picture and have decided on the final dimensions, convert the coloured image into a line drawing (the working design) of the right size.

First obtain a black and white photocopy from your original, scaled to the finished size.

Trace the outline of all the main areas of the picture on to a sheet of plain paper. If you cannot obtain sheets of carbon paper fix the photocopy to a window pane and mount a sheet of tracing or detail paper over the top – the light from outside will allow you to trace the image.

Do not include too much detail. You should aim to simplify the picture to match your skills, without detracting from the overall effect.

You will note that in my interpretation of Norwich Cathedral I have omitted the clouds and some of the finer architectural detail. I have also moved the house at the right of the cathedral into the background.

You could include extra items to improve the overall balance of the picture; a tree in the foreground, to frame a subject, or a figure to add a little bit of life to the picture.

If you do not have access to a photocopier to resize your original image use the grid method of reproducing a line drawing. Draw a grid of equi-spaced vertical and horizontal lines (as in a graph) on your original picture. If you do not want to damage the picture draw the graph on to a sheet of transparent material. Now draw a similar grid, scaled to size for the finished work, on a sheet of plain paper. Use the grid lines as guides and copy across the essential parts of the picture.

Another method is to project a slide on to a piece of paper and trace the image. A photographic enlarger or epidiascope can also be used in a similar manner. The advantage of using these methods is that the projector, etc., can be positioned to give the correct size.

Calculations for enlargements and reductions.

$$\frac{Finished\ size}{Original\ size} \times 100 = Enlargement/reduction$$

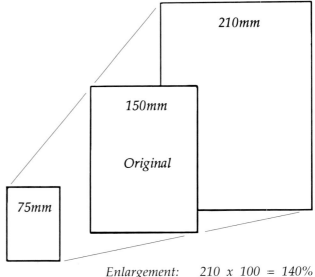

Enlargement: $\frac{210}{150} \times 100 = 140\%$

Reduction: $\frac{75}{150} \times 100 = 50\%$

Original photograph with a grid drawn on to a transparent overlay.

Draw a grid at a larger scale on to a sheet of paper and then draw the working design.

Finished picture reproduced at full size.

Veneers

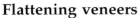

This veneer must be flattened before use.

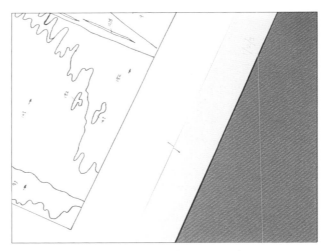

Draw a registration mark on drawing and waster.

Flattening veneers

Some veneers are not very flat when purchased and they could prove difficult to use. Flatten veneers by soaking them in water and then leaving them in a press or under a heavy weight until they are dry.

Preparing the waster

A waster acts as a temporary backing veneer out of which the initial windows are cut. Cut a piece of thin card about 50mm (2in) wider and longer than the finished size of your picture.

Position the working design drawing on the waster and secure at the top edge with some adhesive tape. Draw a short diagonal line across the bottom edge of the line drawing on to the waster. This line provides a registration mark for correct alignment of your picture as it progresses.

Face side of veneers

When a veneer is made, knife marks are sometimes left on one side of the veneer, and this side is usually rougher than the other. It is the smooth side which is used as the face side.

If you have difficulty in deciding which is which, try flexing the veneer along the grain. You will find that it bends more easily in one direction than the other, as illustrated (right). The face side is uppermost in the direction of most bend.

Veneers bend easily when the face side is uppermost.

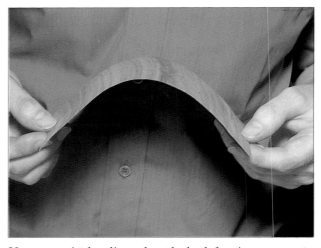

Veneers resist bending when the back face is uppermost.

Simple cutting techniques

Before starting your first picture, get used to handling your knife and practise your cutting techniques on some thin card. When you are happy with this first technique, try cutting some shapes out of a piece of veneer: a square, a triangle and a circle.

Squares and gentle curves

Hold the knife handle at about 45° up from the horizontal, with your wrist resting on the cutting board. Lightly draw the knife towards you, making a score in the veneer. Turn the veneer round and repeat on the other sides. Do not try to cut through the veneer in one go, as this will result in broken blades and lost temper. Continue by making several stroking cuts to each side until you have cut the veneer all the way through.

Triangles

The angles of a triangle mean that, no matter where you place the shape relative to the grain, at least one side will always be at an acute angle to the grain. This is not too much of a problem when cutting a triangular hole, but when you are cutting a triangular insert the grain will tend to split and break away at the corner. To avoid this, place a piece of low-tack adhesive tape at each corner before cutting out the shape to hold the veneer together until it has been inserted and glued into position. Always cut away from the narrow points on the design.

Circles and tight curves

When cutting circles, hold the handle at a steeper angle and use shorter strokes. For very tight curves hold the knife almost vertically and use stab strokes. This method is also used when cutting across the grain of some very hard woods.

Hold the knife at about 45° for straight lines.

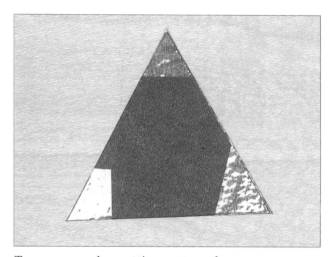
Tape corners when cutting acute angles.

Hold the knife upright when cutting circles.

19

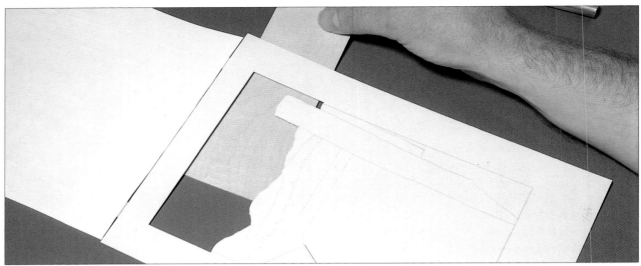

Cutting windows allows you to choose the right veneer.

Cutting windows and inserts

The most popular method of construction for marquetry pictures is called the window method. You cut out a shape in one veneer (a window) and use its edges as a guide for cutting an insert. This method allows you to see the effect of a piece of veneer through the window and so to choose the right veneer or grain for the insert.

A scalpel blade is chamfered on both sides to provide a keen cutting edge. If you hold the knife so that the blade is vertical and make a cut through a veneer the cut edges on either side of the blade will be tapered.

Cuts made with an upright blade will result in poor joints between pieces. You must try to obtain a vertical cut on both the inside edges of the window and the outside edges of the insert.

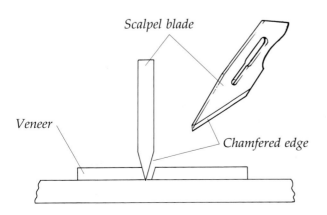

In the following exercise I show you how to achieve a good vertical cut, using a square-shaped window and insert.

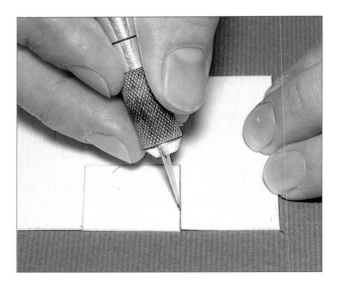

1. First, draw the shape on to one piece of veneer and score lightly over the pencil lines. Hold the knife so that the blade is tilted towards the window side of the shape and cut along the score line. Turn the veneer and repeat for the other lines of the shape.

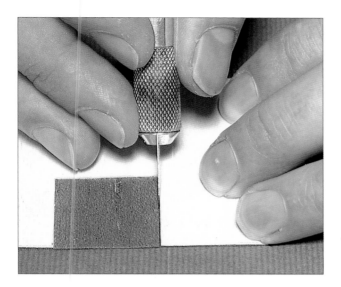

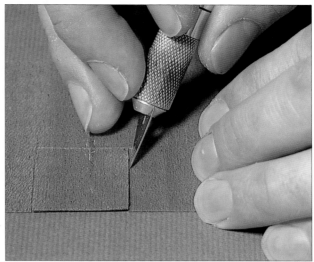

2. Place a contrasting veneer underneath the window and fix it with pieces of low-tack tape on the back. When you are experienced at doing this, you can omit the tape; finger pressure on the veneer should be enough to stop any movement. Hold the knife with the blade just off the vertical and score the shape of the window on the contrast veneer.

3. Remove the marked veneer and, holding the knife so that the blade is tilted towards the outside edge of the insert, cut through as before. Place the insert into the window and hold it in place by rubbing a small amount of PVA glue into the joints on the back face of the veneers.

Common faults

Most of your early errors will be associated with dents, cutting techniques, tape marks, blisters and sanding; they should all be eliminated with practice. Always rectify a fault as soon as possible.

Dents
Treat any indentations in the surface of a veneer with a drop of water, to make the fibres swell and draw them back up to the surface, and then apply heat from an iron on a low setting.

Cutting
If you make a bad job of cutting out a shape throw it away and start again – bad joins between veneers do spoil the overall effect.

If the fault is just a knife slip, put a drop of water on the cut to swell the fibres.

If, when cutting a window, you accidentally score a piece of veneer across the grain, try making several light scoring strokes of the knife with the grain to mask out the offending line.

Tape marks
Some types of sticky tapes leave a residue on the picture which must be removed before finishing. Use a cellulose thinner and scrape them off while still wet. Do not use a cellulose thinner with contact adhesives as the veneers may lift.

Blisters
Blisters are usually caused by patchy gluing and must be treated before the picture is sanded. Others are created by using veneers that are not

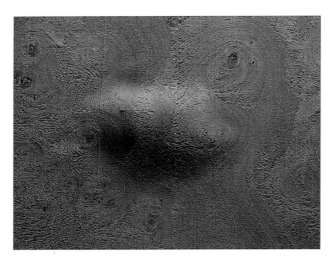

Blister caused by patchy application of glue.

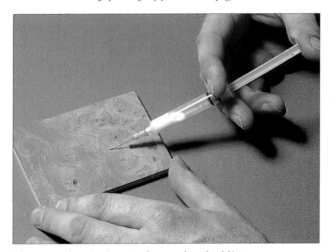

Use a syringe to insert glue under the blister.

perfectly flat or by removing a picture from the press before the glue is thoroughly dry.

Some glues can be remelted by using a domestic iron, at the lowest heat setting, and the blister flattened under pressure until the glue has reset. If this method is not successful split the blister with a knife, along the grain, and push more glue under the veneer with the blade of a knife. Alternatively, use a syringe to inject glue beneath the blister. Always put the repaired picture into the press again until the glue has set.

Sanding faults

If you work one area of the picture too much you can sand right through the veneer, especially if there was a slight blister in the vicinity. However, you can salvage the picture.

Carefully cut round the damaged piece of veneer, make a slit in the centre, slide the knife under the veneer and remove it.

Make a pencil rubbing of the shape on a piece of paper and trace it through on to a new piece of veneer. Cut out the veneer and glue into position.

Sanding over a slight blister wears through the veneer.

Make a pencil rubbing of the damaged shape.

MAKING A PICTURE

In this chapter I take you, step by step, through the complete procedure for making a marquetry picture. I have used one of my own photographs as the basis for the design, and you will note that although I have left out some of the more intricate detail, the overall effect is retained.

The working design

Decide on the finished size of the picture, bearing in mind the factors mentioned on page 16. The full-size pattern opposite measures 134 x 202mm (5¼ x 8in) so, allowing for a 39mm (1½in) border all round, you will need a baseboard that measures 212 x 280mm (8¼ x 11in).

Use one of the methods described on page 16 to produce a line drawing to scale. For this exercise I made a scaled-up black and white photocopy from my original photograph and then traced through the design. You will note that I left out the small dinghy moored alongside the subject boat, the two sets of handrails and the name of the boat. I also simplified the reflections in the foreground and the detail inside the cabin.

Mark the drawing with arrows to indicate the grain direction of major veneer sections.

The original colour photograph.

24

Full-size black-and-white photocopy and the finished working design drawing.

Choosing the veneers

I used the nineteen different veneers shown opposite to make this picture. I chose ones that reflect, as near as possible, the colours and patterns of the original photograph, but you can substitute a completely different colour palette.

I always find it useful to write out a numerical list of the veneers used on a picture; I then add the numbers on to the working design drawing for reference.

1. *Magnolia*
2. *Pommelle*
3. *Harewood, light/silver*
4. *Sapele*
5. *Birch, ice*
6. *Teak*
7. *Walnut, European*
8. *Sycamore*
9. *Makore*
10. *Mahogany, Honduras*
11. *Oak, figured*
12. *Walnut, burr*
13. *Poplar, burr*
14. *Walnut, American*
15. *Rosewood, Indian*
16. *Ash*
17. *Harewood, mid-grey/slate*
18. *Chestnut, sweet*
19. *Ash, burr*

Add the veneer numbers to the design drawing.

Making the background

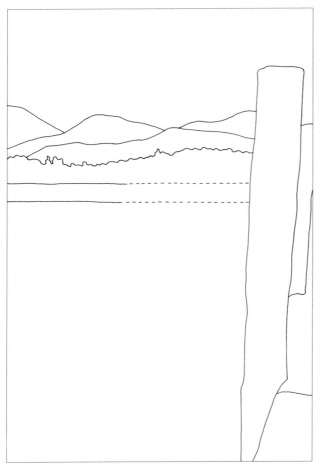

Trace the background details on to the waster.

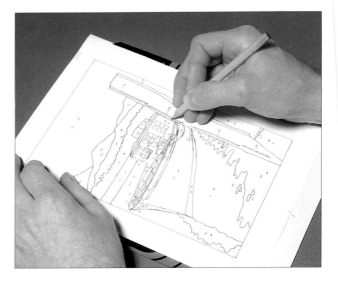

1. Prepare the waster as described on page 18 and then trace out the background areas of the picture as shown in the diagram (left).

2. Lift up the line drawing and, allowing about 3mm (¹/₈in) overlap beyond the border of the design, cut out the sky-section window from the waster. The small border will be trimmed back later on completion of the picture.

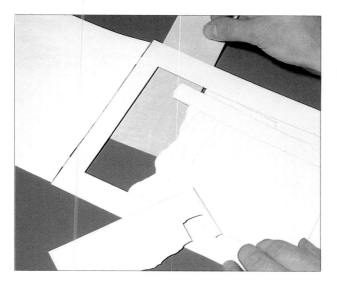

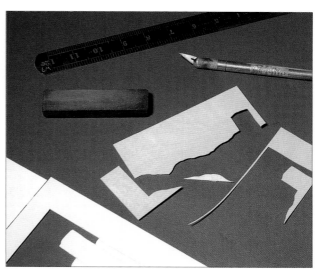

3. Place the sky veneer (No. 8) underneath the window and move it around to obtain the most suitable position. The advantage of using the window method is obvious; you can place different pieces of veneer beneath the window and select the most suitable before cutting.

5. Remove the veneer and, using the cutting technique for inserts, cut out the sky shape. Remember to use several light cuts rather than trying to cut through the veneer in one go.

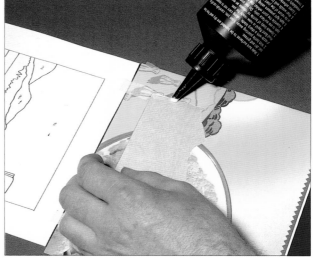

4. When you have chosen your veneer, tape it lightly to the underside of the waster and then score round the edge of the window on to the veneer below.

6. Turn the waster over, place the veneer into the window opening and apply a small amount of PVA glue along the border edges.

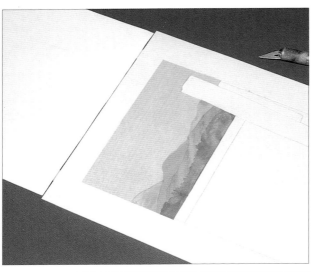

7. Repeat stages 2–6 for the hill shapes (Nos. 13, 1 and 18) and the trees (No. 19). Stick some low-tack tape to the tree line on veneer Nos. 18 and 19 and use very short strokes to cut the shape.

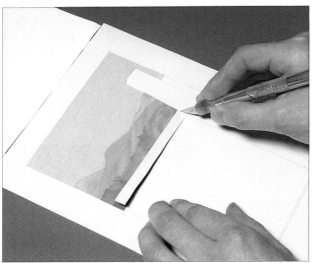

8. Cut out the background water shape from the waster, noting that it includes the area behind the boat, and fit veneer No. 8.

9. Cut out and fit the foreground water veneer No. 1. Select a veneer which has a grain that gets progressively wider from one side to the other and place it with the narrow grain at the top. Complete the background adding the basic jetty details with veneer Nos. 7, 11 and 16.

Adding the boat design

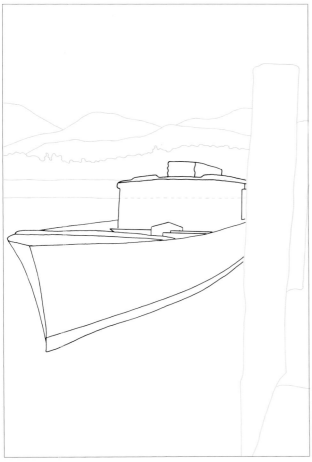

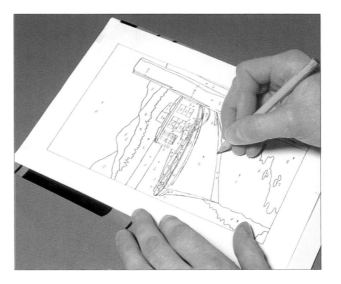

1. Replace the line drawing over the waster and background veneers, align registration marks and tape it down. Trace through the outline of the boat as shown in the diagram (left).

Trace through the outline of the boat.

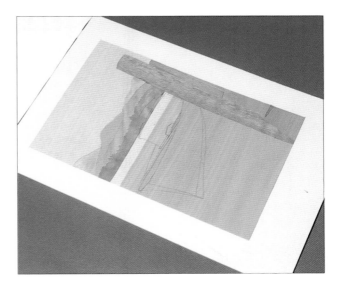

2. Redraw the border line on to the background veneers.

3. Cut out and fit the hull sections of the boat (veneer Nos. 15, 10 and 9). Rosewood (No. 15) is hard to cut so hold the knife almost vertical and stab through the veneer, gradually moving along the line, and then use short strokes to complete the cut. Cut out and fit the cabin (veneer No. 10); save the pieces of background water veneers (No. 1 and 8) to use in the windows later. Keep any larger pieces of waste veneer – they always come in useful for other pictures.

4. Cut and fit the remaining pieces of the deck and cabin roof.

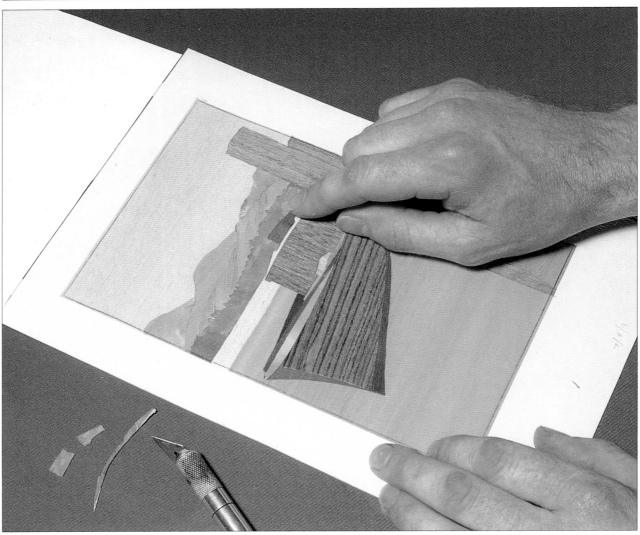

Completing the design

1. Replace the line drawing and now trace through the window details on the boat and the foreground water reflections as shown above.

2. Cut out the cabin windows using the pieces of veneer Nos. 1 and 8 removed earlier. Check that the grain matches and follows through each window. Cut out and fit the veneers for the foreground water reflections (Nos. 6 and 14).

3. Trace through the fine detail on the boat, the foreground and the jetty, and then cut out and fit the veneers.

4. The basic picture is now complete. Hold the picture up to the light and check for any large gaps – replace any badly fitting pieces.

5. Look at the colour, tone and grain – wipe a little sanding sealer over the picture to bring out the colour – and change any unsuitable pieces.

Making a border

1. Trim the finished picture to the drawn border mark, making sure that the sides are square to one another. For the border of this picture cut four lengths, 6mm (¼in) wide, from veneer No. 6; four lengths, 3mm (⅛in) wide, from veneer No. 8; and four lengths, 32mm (1¼in) wide, from veneer No. 7. Make the lengths slightly longer than the finished picture size. If possible use four consecutive leaves of veneer, which should be kept the same way round.

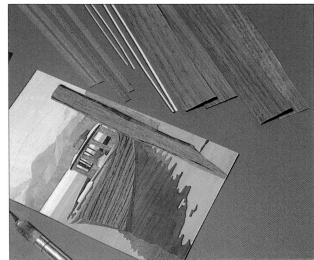

2. Using low-tack tape, attach the first set of veneers (No. 6) around the edges of the picture and mitre the corners by cutting across the intersecting veneers.

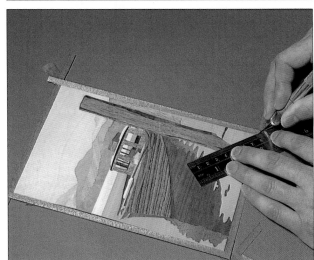

3. Fit the stringer veneers (No. 8) around the outside. Complete the border with the third set of veneers (No. 7). Tape the first short piece to the top of the picture, then turn the second piece over and tape it at the bottom. Repeat with the other two borders at the sides. Mitre the corners and hold them together with tape, then turn the whole picture over and glue the border pieces in place.

Mounting the picture

1. Cut a piece of MDF approximately 6mm (¼in) shorter and narrower than the finished picture. Cut a backing veneer (No. 14) – to stop the finished picture from warping – the same size as the picture. Cut four lengths of edge veneer (No. 14) slightly wider than the thickness of the mounting board.

2. Spread a thin layer of PVA glue on the baseboard and allow it to become tacky. Position the baseboard on the backing veneer. Cover it with a sheet of polythene and several layers of newspaper, and put it into a press veneer-face downwards, so that any glue which is squeezed out does not run down the sides. After about fifteen minutes in the press, check the veneer for blisters; remove these by wiping a domestic iron on a low heat-setting over the affected area. Return the panel to the press and leave for a further three to four hours.

3. Remove the board from the press, trim off the surplus veneer and sandpaper the edges flush.

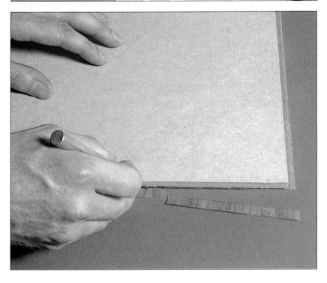

4. Apply a layer of water-based contact adhesive to the top edge of the baseboard and one of the shorter pieces of edge veneer. Let it become tacky and then lay the veneer on the edge of the board.

5. Use the handle of your knife or any other smooth piece of material to apply pressure to help make a good seal. Repeat with the bottom edge strip. Let the adhesive set, then trim off the ends and repeat for the two side edges. Trim off surplus veneer and sand the edges flush with the mounting board. If you decide to frame your picture you can leave out the edging strips.

6. Glue the finished picture on to the baseboard in a similar way to that described in stages 2 and 3. Take extra care in lining up the corners with the mitres on the picture. Leave the picture for a day or two for the glue to cure and then trim off the surplus veneer and sand the edges flush.

Finishing the picture

1. Use a flat-bladed scraper to remove shavings from the thicker veneers in the picture, working with the grain. If you do not have a scraper you can use one of the coarser grit papers to achieve the same effect.

2. Use a pad made up of cotton wool wrapped in a cotton cloth to rub on a couple of coats of sanding sealer, allowing the first coat to dry before applying the second. The sealer fills in the open pores of the veneer and prevents the dust generated by sanding from filling them in and causing discoloration.

3. Sand the surface of the picture, starting with a coarse 180 grit paper wrapped around a sanding block. Work in the direction in which the majority of veneer grains occur. Do not let the block go over the edges of the picture. Use a soft brush to remove the dust from the picture at frequent intervals. When the surface feels smooth, change to a 220 grit paper and then follow with a 280 grit paper. Apply six to eight coats of sanding sealer as described in stage 2. Rub down with a 320 grit paper and then apply another six coats of sanding sealer. Rub down lightly with the 320 grit paper then apply a couple of coats of siliconised furniture wax and burnish with a soft cloth.

DECORATED OBJECTS

A marquetry design can be used to decorate items such as a small box or a clock. You can also use your skills to produce other objects, and in this chapter I show you how to cut veneers into geometric patterns (a method known as parquetry) to make a chessboard and a set of coasters.

Making a chessboard

1. Cut two contrasting veneers into strips of the required width. Make them eight times longer than the width plus a small amount for trimming. You will need five lengths of the light veneer and four of the darker one. Arrange alternate colours and then join together using tape.

3. Move alternate strips to make the chessboard pattern. Fix with tape and trim off the extra squares of light veneers at each side.

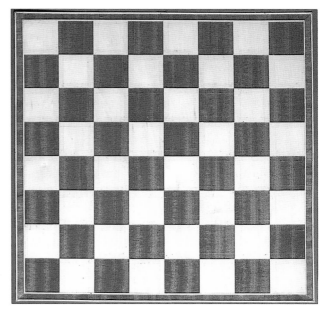

2. Use a set square to draw a pencil line along one of the edges at a true 90° to the lengths of veneers and trim off the excess veneer. Measure and cut eight parallel strips across the grain.

4. Measure and cut the banding and stringer veneers and, using the techniques described on page 35, complete the basic pattern. Mount the completed design and then sand and seal the surface as described on page 38.

You can make a more impressive chessboard by adding a border around the basic design. Make the border slightly larger on two ends and incorporate some form of marquetry or parquetry design.

Diamonds and triangles

Diamonds and triangles require slightly more attention to accuracy than the simple squares of a chessboard. Cut strips of contrasting veneers and join them together with tape. Cut across the strips at 60° rather than at right-angles to produce diamond shapes. Cut each diamond in half; across the length to give shallow triangles, and across the width to give equilateral triangles. Both shapes are very useful for making numerous geometric designs. A simple cutting jig will improve your accuracy when making these shapes (see opposite).

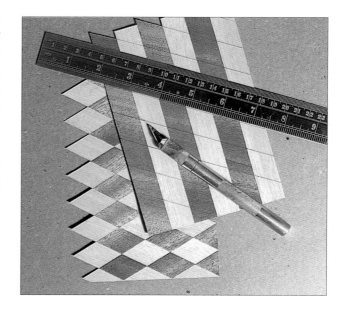

Making a set of coasters

The basic requirements for making a set of coasters are much the same as those for a marquetry picture, except that the baseboard is usually thinner – I use 6mm (¼in) MDF. Contact adhesive, melamine sealer and baize are the only other requirements.

The finished size of the coaster shown below is 100mm (4in) square, with the corners rounded with a radius of 12mm (½in). The design is set within a 76mm (3in) diameter circle.

The design used on the coasters is an eight-pointed star, made up from sixteen individual triangles the acute angles of which are 22.5° (360 divided by 16). This angle can be constructed using a set square and a pair of compasses (see 'Bisecting an angle' below).

The pattern can be made up using the window method described earlier in the book but greater accuracy, and a more symmetrical finish, is achieved if a simple cutting jig is used.

Increase the size of the design and you can make a matching set of table mats.

Finished coaster with an eight-pointed star design.

Bisecting an angle

Use a set square to draw an angle of 45° and then use a pair of compasses to bisect this angle. Place the compass on point A and draw an arc to cut

the lines at B and C. Now place the compass point on B and draw another arc. Repeat at point C. Draw a line between points A and D; the angle now formed is 22.5°.

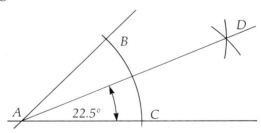

Making a jig

Use MDF or similar material for making the baseboard and the jig shape. Cut out a rectangular shape for the baseboard and a right-angled triangle, with one angle cut at precisely 22.5°, for the jig (any error at this point will be multiplied by a factor of 16 in the finished design). Cut a right angle in the hypotenuse (longest side) of the jig piece, making the long side equal to the longest length of each individual triangle in the design. Glue and screw the jig to the base.

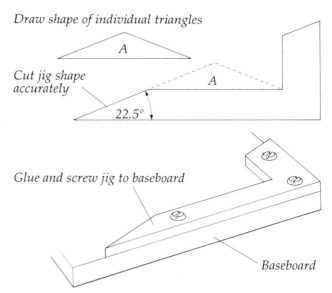

Draw shape of individual triangles

Cut jig shape accurately

Glue and screw jig to baseboard

Baseboard

Making the basic design

Select two contrasting veneers that have a plain or straight grain – for this example I used teak and horse chestnut.

1. Cut parallel strips the same width as the height of the triangle. Put one strip in the jig and cut a diagonal line using a steel rule. Turn the strip over, insert the pointed end into the jig as shown and make another cut to form a triangle. Cut eight pieces from each of the two veneers.

3. Position and glue each triangle in turn to complete the design.

2. Draw the design on to the background veneer and carefully cut out the complete star shape.

4. Cut out and fit the background pieces. Use a heat-resistant contact adhesive to stick a backing veneer, then an edge strip (applied as a single piece) and finally the design itself to the baseboard. An ideal surface finish would be melamine, which is water- and heat-resistant. Apply baize to the bottom.

Selection of geometric designs for coasters. Note the effect (at top) of reversing the contrast of the veneers.

Decorating other objects

Although marquetry is an ancient craft, its use as an art form for wall-hanging pictures only became popular at the beginning of the twentieth century. Before that date it had been used mainly to decorate items of furniture so it can be said that it is more traditional to use your marquetry design to decorate an object. Today such this type of use is known as applied marquetry.

To make a piece of furniture and decorate it with marquetry would be a major project, but there are many smaller items to which marquetry can be applied. Jewellery boxes are very popular, as are clocks, lamp bases, coasters and table mats, to name but a few.

Some objects may require a little skill in woodwork, although smaller items such as boxes can be bought ready made. Use the same process as for pictures to cover them; apply veneer to the bottom first, then the sides and finally the top. For this type of work I recommend the use of a contact adhesive or a sheet of glue film.

When using contact adhesives always follow the manufacturer's instructions. Most glues of this type require layers to be applied to both surfaces. These must then be allowed to dry out before sticking the pieces together.

This pretty jewellery box started as a plain wooden box.

I designed and made the basic case of these clocks in ceramic and then applied a decorative design using veneers.

OTHER TECHNIQUES

In this chapter I show you how to add a three-dimensional effect to your pictures and how to deal with fine detail, and I also suggest alternative methods of creating borders.

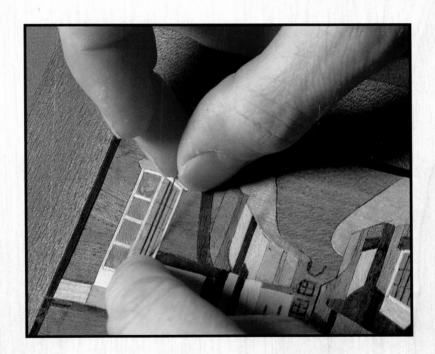

Sand shading

Sand shading is a technique of colouring veneers and has been used in marquetry work for over five hundred years. It is still used today and examples can be seen on the shell and fan inlay motifs which are used extensively on commercial products.

Sand shading results in a gradual change in tone and gives depth to flower petals, for example; it is also useful for creating shadows and the illusion of roundness on curves, etc.

You will require a small metal dish (a baking tin is ideal) filled with about 35mm (1½in) of silver sand, which is available from garden centres or pet shops. You will also need a heat source (a gas burner or an electric hotplate) , a pair of tweezers and a spoon.

Heat the silver sand on the gas burner. Experiment with scraps of waste veneer to get to know the correct temperature.

Hold a piece of veneer with tweezers and push it well into the sand – do not let it touch the bottom of the tin as it will char. Leave for about five seconds, withdraw and check the colour. A five-second insertion should give a reasonable shade effect. If the veneer starts to char reduce the heat. Leave the veneer in the sand slightly longer to achieve darker shades; shorter periods will give lighter shades.

The veneer will shrink slightly when inserted into the hot sand – if you are using the window method of construction, use a piece of veneer slightly larger than the window and then finally cut the shaded veneer to fit.

When shading is required in the middle of a piece of veneer, use a small spoon to pile some hot sand on the part to be shaded and tip it off again after a few seconds. You can produce a shaded shape on the veneer using a mask with a window cut in it.

Insert the veneer into the sand for about five seconds.

Shade a piece of veneer that is slightly larger than the window and then trim to fit.

Other forms of shading

Shading can also be achieved using a domestic iron or a pyrography pen. Pens are available with different point sizes to give a range of effects from very fine lines to large areas of solid/graduated tone.

Other methods of changing the tone or colour of the veneer include bleaching, dyeing and dusting. These techniques are quite complicated and I suggest that they be left to serious marquetarians and commercial companies.

Completed picture, reproduced at full size, in which the petals of the flowers have all been sand shaded.

Fine detail

Some designs may require the use of very fine detail – for example, the outlines of window panes or the rigging on ships. There are two methods that can be used.

Pyrography

A simple method of dealing with fine detail is to use a pyrography pen, with a fine point, to burn the shape on to a veneer. I used this method for the rigging on the mast and sails of the Norfolk wherry (see page 63), a detail from which is shown right.

Cutting slivers

For the more adventurous thin strips of wood (slivers) can be inserted into the background veneers.

1. Use a straight-edge and knife to cut a strip, as thin as possible, from the edge of a sheet of veneer. If necessary, reduce the width of the strip by flattening it with the handle of the knife.

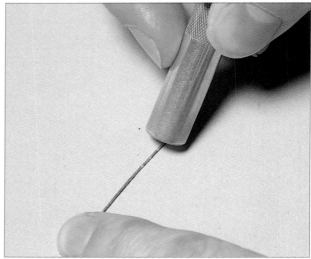

2. Cut a slit in the background veneer, the thickness of the blade, and slide in the prepared sliver.

Borders

It is important to strike a balance between the border and the subject of any picture; the eye has to be drawn in towards the design. Normally plain straight-grained veneers are used for the borders, perhaps with contrasting stringers, as illustrated on page 39.

Cross-banding

An alternative method is to cut the veneer across the grain into strips to form cross-banding. Eight pieces are cut using consecutive leaves of veneers opened like the pages of a book. They are cut at 45 or 90° to the picture. Strengthen the veneer with tape when cutting across the grain, and always cut away from the point on the corners to avoid splitting. An example of 90° cross-banding is given on page 49.

Inlays

Cut a window out of a large sheet of veneer and glue in the completed design. When mounted and finished the picture will have the appearance of being inlaid into a piece of solid wood.

Framing

If you frame your picture try to match the frame to the border veneer. Keep the shape simple and use natural colours which enhance the overall effect. Allow time for the surface finish to sink before fixing a frame (see page 50).

45° cross-banding is made from eight pieces of veneer.

Keep the shape of frames simple.

Create an inlay by using a border cut from a single piece of veneer. Cut a window and fit your design.

51

Alternative finishes

A marquetry picture can be finished in a number of ways; matt, semi-matt or gloss. The semi-matt finish was used in the step-by-step instructions for the boat picture (see page 38). The type of finish used is down to personal choice although items such as a table top, coasters or table mats do need to be heat- and water-resistant. Melamine or a plastic coating would be suitable in this case.

Matt finish

A matt finish is achieved in much the same way as that described on page 38 except that wax polish would not be applied. Alternatively finish the picture with a catalyst cold cure matt finish.

Gloss finish

A high gloss finish is often preferred by marquetarians. Probably one of the easiest methods to attain this is to use a two-part catalyst lacquer. Several coats are applied and then burnished with a paste to provide a mirror-like gloss.

The more traditional way is to use French polish but this method does require a certain amount of skill to get a good finish. However, there are some DIY-type French polish kits available which contain a polish and a finishing solution. The polish is applied as a series of coats each of which is rubbed down before the next is applied. The finishing solution is used to burnish the surface to the required degree of gloss.

Sinking

No matter how much attention is given to the finishing process 'sinking' will always occur – the sealers and waxes sink into the grain and joints of the veneers. When it becomes very visible sand down the surface again, apply a few more coats of sealer, polish or plastic coating and then finish as usual.

The surface of this coaster has sunk and exposed the grain details. It must be sanded and finished again.

GALLERY

In this chapter I have included a selection of pictures to show the wide range of subjects that lend themselves to marquetry. Each picture is accompanied by a short caption to explain particular aspects of the design. I have also included a number of working design drawings for you to enlarge and use for your own pictures. I have left out details of the veneers that I used on purpose; one of the most fascinating aspects of this craft is choosing veneers for their colour and grain pattern to suit the design.

The Grange, Borrowdale

Gallery

Bridge House, Ambleside

Brick or stone buildings can be difficult to portray in marquetry because the scale is usually too small to cut out each individual brick or stone. I tend to outline parts of the structure either by inserting thin slivers of veneer or by using a pyrography pen, with a fine point, to burn the detail on to the surface.

Size: 150 x 100mm (6 x 4in)

York Minster

*Planetree or grey planetree (a harewood) veneers have fleck-type figuring
which give the impression of pebbles and gravel. I used these veneers,
together with slate harewood, for the cobblestones and pavement in this
picture. I also used other harewoods for the walls of York Minster.*

Size (including frame): 275 x 225mm (11 x 9in)

Thornton-le-Dale

Trees, shrubs and flowers are best kept simple. Do not try and cut out individual leaves until you are used to cutting intricate shapes. Let the grain of a veneer create the effect; many veneers can be used for this purpose, especially the burr veneers.

I used the original photograph as a guide for the freehand drawing of the working design. Working this way gives you the freedom to change or simplify some of the detail. You can use all or only part of a photograph, and you can add detail to give more interest. Note how I have changed the perspective of the building.

Size: 125 x 175mm (5 x 7in)

57

The Shambles, York

Timber-framed buildings are a feature of this narrow street in the city of York and are particularly suitable subjects for marquetry.

For this picture I made an enlarged photocopy from the photograph and then traced through the detail to create the working design. This method ensured that the perspective was correct, a very important factor when buildings are the focal point of a picture.

Consideration must also be given to the choice of colours; there is a very restricted palette and, unless you resort to dyed veneers, you must remember that there are no natural veneers in the blue and green areas of the spectrum. This can mean that you will not be able to copy colours exactly, especially bright daylight colours. However, if you imagine the picture taken late in the afternoon, many of the more vivid colours will become muted to the yellows, reds and browns of a wide range of veneers.

Size: 265 x 185mm (10$\frac{1}{2}$ x 7$\frac{1}{4}$in)

Cley Mill, Norfolk

You will note that the original black-and-white magazine picture of Cley Mill had two boats in the foreground. I thought that they clashed with the subject, especially the masts which protruded across the sails of the mill. When developing the working design I left out these boats completely but included a simple dinghy and two mooring posts to give a more pleasing composition.

Another version of this picture, using different veneers and a small sailing boat instead of the dinghy, is shown on the front cover of this book

Size (including border): 340 x 215mm (13^1/$_2$ x 8^1/$_2$in)

Pull's Ferry, Norwich

It can be very difficult to get depth into a picture. I have attempted to create depth by choosing my veneers very carefully. The most distant tree is the lightest shade and I have gradually made the trees darker as they approach the foreground.

Size: 125 x 175mm (5 x 7in)

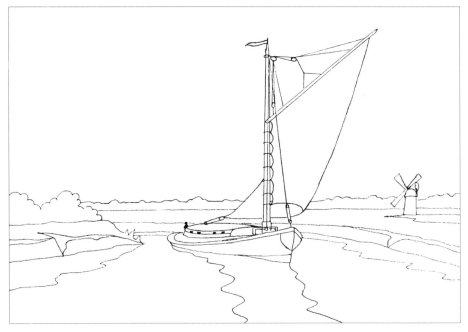

Norfolk Wherry

Sailing boats make a very simple yet effective design for marquetry pictures. Although I have used my pyrography pen to show the rigging in this picture, you could try inserting slivers to achieve a more satisfying result.

Harewood, with its grey tones, is very useful for depicting water.

Size: 125 x 175mm (5 x 7in)

Desert

This is my interpretation of a desert scene. It is very simple in design with very few intricate cuts. However, I was able to create the effect of moving sands and dunes by careful selection of wood grains. I inserted the dead tree to provide contrast and a focal point.

Size (including border): 305 x 215mm (12 x 8$\frac{1}{2}$in)

Seaweed

Another easy design to construct. I used a light contrasting border, with a narrow dark stringer, both for this design and for the desert scene above. Use sanding sealer before starting the sanding operation to avoid getting dust from the dark veneers in the pores of the lighter ones.

Size (including border): 325 x 220mm (12$\frac{3}{4}$ x 8$\frac{5}{8}$in)

64

Sunset

Most of the mood of this picture is created by the choice of colour and grain.
Size (including border): 205 x 150mm (8 x 6in)

Owl

A burr veneer came in useful for depicting the craters on the moon. I used a dark harewood to suggest a night sky and provide a contrast to the colours of the owl.

Size (including border): 250 x 205mm (10 x 8in)

Robin

In this picture I extended the branch of the tree over the border to give the illusion of extra depth. I have also used a wooden frame to give a final edge.

Size (including the frame): 242 x 192mm (9^1/$_2$ x 7^1/$_2$in)

Autumn Girl

Browns, reds and yellows predominate in the marquetry palette, and we associate these colours with autumn. It is often much easier to change the season depicted in a picture rather than struggle to achieve the brightness of summer colours.

I have given the design a rounded top and 'inlaid' it in a border cut from a single sheet of veneer. You could be more adventurous and make the border into an arch or window.

Size (including border):
340 x 200mm (13¹/₄ x 8in)

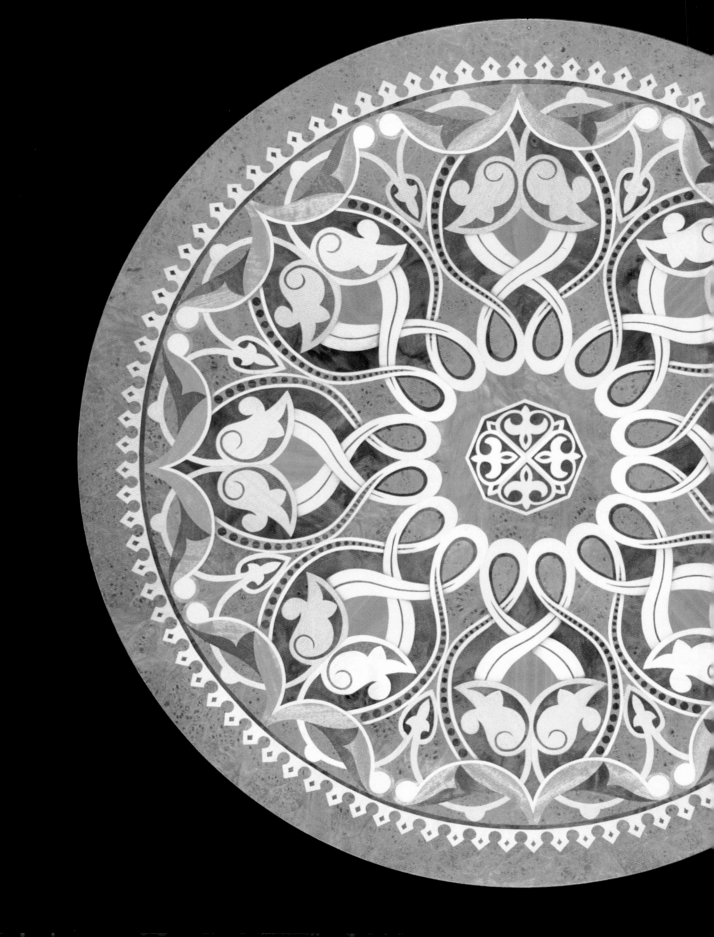

Table

When you have completed a few of the more simple projects you might want to try something a bit more complex such as a table top. On a complicated design, especially for circular patterns, it is easier to split the overall design into sections. I made this table top in eight identical sections; I produced photocopies of the basic design and stuck them together with tape to ensure that I had a perfect fit. I then made each section in turn in the usual way and joined them as I worked round the table.

The influence for your design can come from a variety of sources – mediaeval, Greek and Gothic patterns can often be found in historical books.

Size: 760mm (30in) diameter

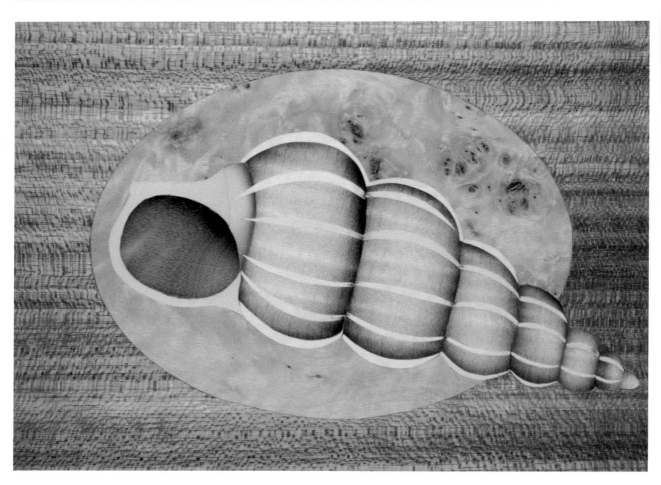

Shell

Sand shading is a useful technique and can be used to indicate curves and shadows. I used this method quite extensively to bring out the beautiful curvature of this shell.

Size: 125 x 165mm (5 x 6$\frac{1}{2}$in)

Water Lily

Dyed woods can be used to good effect, especially where a modern style is required. They are also very suitable for cartoon characters. However, I would still recommend that they be used sparingly.

Size (including border):
170 x 215mm (6$\frac{3}{4}$ x 8$\frac{1}{2}$in)

THE MARQUETRY PALETTE

Wood can be divided into two groups – softwood and hardwood. Softwoods come from coniferous (evergreen) trees and are used extensively in the construction and paper-making industries, but seldom for the supply of veneers. Hardwoods are generally obtained from deciduous trees (they shed their leaves each year) and provide most of the veneers used in marquetry.

However, the terms 'soft' and 'hard' have nothing to do with the ease of cutting. Some hardwoods are much softer, and easier to cut, than softwoods and vice versa. With a little practice you will soon come to know the woods which are easier to cut.

Veneers from across the world

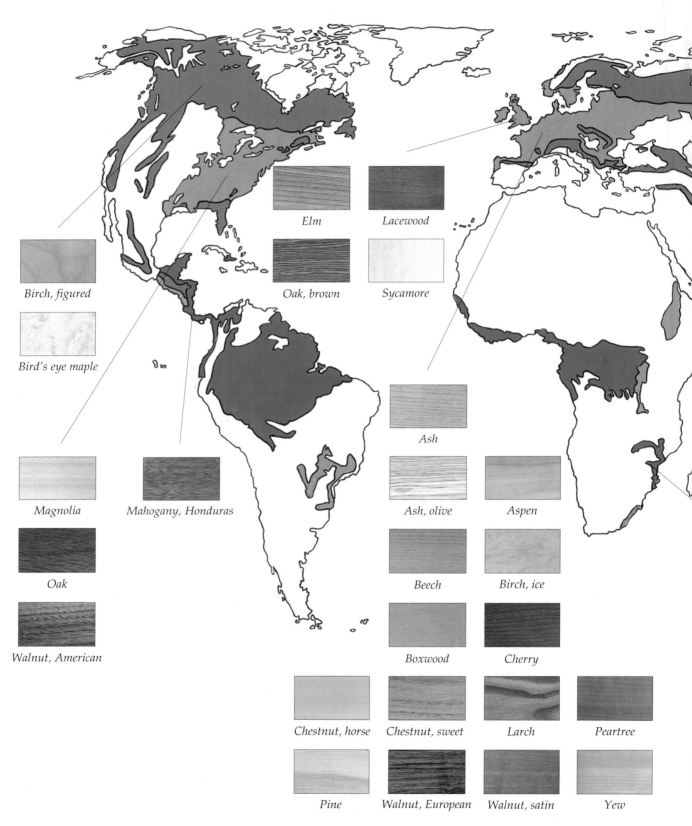

Birch, figured

Bird's eye maple

Elm

Lacewood

Oak, brown

Sycamore

Magnolia

Mahogany, Honduras

Ash

Ash, olive

Aspen

Oak

Beech

Birch, ice

Walnut, American

Boxwood

Cherry

Chestnut, horse

Chestnut, sweet

Larch

Peartree

Pine

Walnut, European

Walnut, satin

Yew

Broadleaf
Coniferous
Monsoon
Tropical
Sub-tropical

Teak

Makore

Pommelle   *Sapele*

Walnut, Australian

Conservation

The subject of conservation provokes much discussion throughout the world as many of the most beautiful veneers come from rare trees. Up to 95 per cent of the trees felled in the rainforests are burnt on the spot, simply to provide access for the removal of the few used for the production of wooden furniture, etc. Some of this timber does end up as veneers, but it is more in the way of a by-product. Much is now being done to try and eliminate this wanton waste.

Importers of veneers are now endeavouring to obtain their stocks from renewable sources; teak, Indian rosewood and some species of mahogany are now supplied in this way. Many of the temperate hardwoods, such as ash, beech, birch, oak, sycamore, yew and walnut, are also taken from managed forests.

Cutting wood into veneers

There are many factors which contribute to the eventual pattern of a veneer but the characteristics of a particular wood (its grain and texture), and the method of cutting it are the two most important ones.

Characteristics

One tree can provide a number of veneers, all with different characteristics: straight grain, butt, burr and curl (or crotch) veneers.

Straight grain veneers are cut from a veneer log that is taken from the trunk of a tree, between the root bowl and the first limb.

Butt veneers are more highly figured and are taken from the area nearest the root base, just above ground level.

Groups of buds which fail to develop form knobbly growths on the trunk of the tree and provide **burr veneers**. When cut the growths show as numerous knot-like formations on a highly figured background grain.

Curl veneers are cut from the junction where a branch protrudes from the tree trunk.

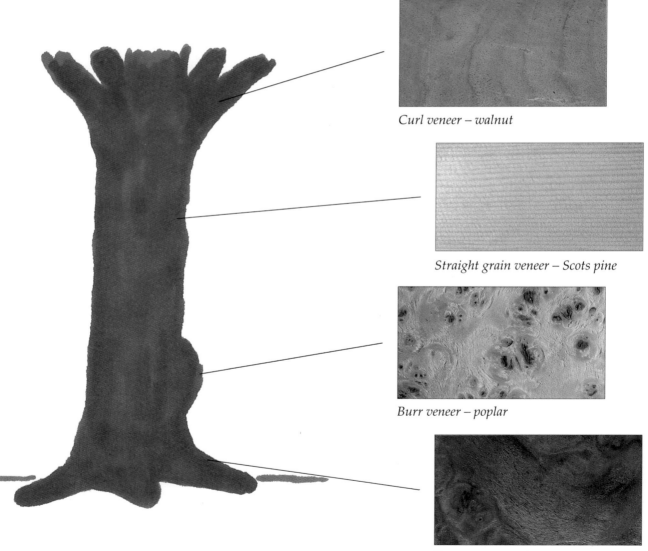

Curl veneer – walnut

Straight grain veneer – Scots pine

Burr veneer – poplar

Butt veneer – walnut

Types of cut

There are several ways in which a log can be cut into veneers; each type giving different grain patterns.

For the construction of plywood, and for the production of a few decorative veneers – bird's eye maple and Mazur birch, for example – a **rotary cut** is used. A log is first peeled of its bark and soaked in water to soften the wood. It is then mounted on a large lathe and spun against a long blade to produce large sheets of veneer.

Other decorative veneers are produced by cutting a log in half, clamping it to a rotating shaft (stay log) and then slicing it against a blade. A true **half-rotary cut**, producing wide sheets of veneer, takes the first slice from the sapwood side of the log. A **half-rotary back-cut** slices from the heart of the log first and is used when cutting butt and curl veneers.

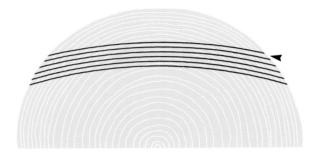

True half-rotary cut takes the first slice from the sapwood side of a log.

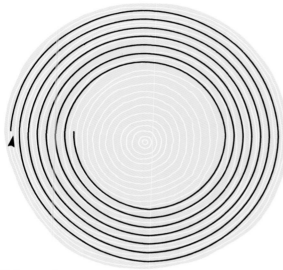

Rotary cut.

Half-rotary back-cut slices from the heartwood.

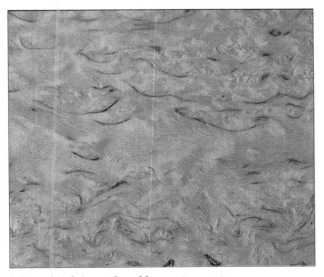

Mazur birch is produced by a rotary cut.

A half-rotary cut gives large sheets of horse chestnut.

Crown cutting (flat slicing) is the method used when cutting ash, elm and walnut, and for the production of burr veneers. The log is cut in half and flat slices taken across its width.

Quarter cutting maximises the striped figuring of some veneers – sapele, for example. A log is cut into quarters (flitches) and slices taken at 90° to the growth rings. Quarter cutting also brings out the medullary rays very well.

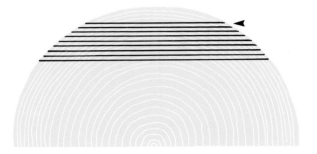

Crown cutting takes flat slices across the width of a log.

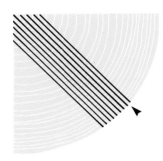

Quarter cutting flitches.

Elm veneers are produced by crown cutting.

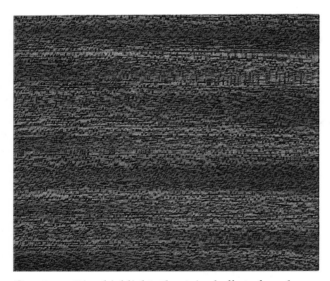

Quarter cutting highlights the striped effect of sapele.

Thicknesses
Veneers can be cut to a variety of thicknesses. Those used in Europe are about 0.7mm ($^1/_{40}$in) thick whilst in the USA 0.9mm ($^1/_{28}$in) is the normal thickness.

Sheet sizes
Sheet sizes vary and can be as long as 5.5 metres (18ft), although for marquetry purposes these are cut down into small lengths.

Other sources of colour

The veneers shown on pages 75 and 76 are just a small selection of the many natural colours that are available. To widen the range of your colour palette chemically treated and dyed woods are also available.

Harewoods
Chemically treated woods are known as harewoods. Certain woods, such as sycamore, are soaked in a solution of ferrous sulphate and water. The chemical reacts with the tannin in the wood to produce a range of shades of grey.

Dyed veneers
A wide range of dyed veneers, in vivid colours, are also available. However, I would suggest that they be used with caution because the colours are very bright and will stand out against those of natural woods and may spoil the overall effect. Some dyes do not penetrate into the veneer and the colour can be affected during the sanding and finishing process. Black is perhaps the most widely used dyed-veneer colour and it is ideal for forming lines and bandings around marquetry pictures.

Borders
A variety of commercially produced borders, inlay bandings and stringers are available in a range of styles and patterns.

Cross-banding made from satinwood, tulipwood and rosewood can also be obtained, and these have a combination of boxwood and dyed-black stringers on each side.

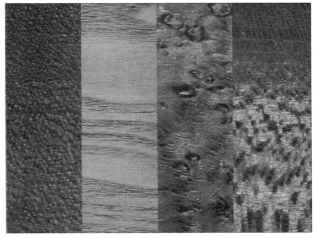
Harewoods give tones of grey.

Dyed woods can look artificial.

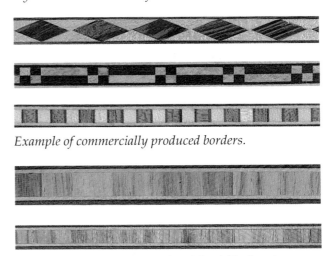
Example of commercially produced borders.

Cross-banding with boxwood and dyed-black stringer.

Index

Bibliography

Campkin, Maria *The Technique of Marquetry* Batsford, London, 1969

Hobbs, Harry Jason *Veneering Simplified* Thames and Hudson, London, 1980

Hobbs & Fitchett *Modern Marquetry Handbook* Thames and Hudson, London, 1980

Jackson, F. Hamilton *Intarsia and Marquetry* Sands & Co., 1903

Lincoln, William A. *The Marquetry Manual* Stobart & Sons, London, 1989

Further reading
The Marquetarian, the quarterly journal of the Marquetry Society.
Art Veneers, a catalogue from The Art Veneers Co. Ltd., Mildenhall, Suffolk.